Parkinson's Disease Diet Cookbook For Seniors

Nutrition Guide and Recipes for Parkinson's Illness Management and Treatment for Older People

Dr. Tate Mandara

Table of Content

INTRODUCTION

Alisson, a senior man in his late 70s, was grappling with the challenges of Parkinson's Disease. His once steady hands had become shaky, and simple tasks like tying shoelaces or enjoying a meal had turned into daily battles. The tremors, stiffness, and unpredictability of the disease were robbing him of his independence.

Then, he discovered the "Parkinson's Diet Cookbook for Seniors." He decided to give it a try. As he started incorporating the carefully crafted recipes into his daily routine, Alisson noticed remarkable changes. The nutrient-packed meals were not only delicious but also made him feel energized. With time, Alisson's symptoms began to ease.

The tremors lessened, and he felt more in control of his body. He noticed improved balance, which was a welcome relief from the fear of falling. The ingredients rich in antioxidants, vitamins, and minerals were nourishing his body, helping to combat the effects of the disease.

Not only did Alisson's physical health improve, but his mental well-being received a boost too. He felt more positive and engaged, ready to tackle life's challenges with newfound determination. The carefully designed diet in the cookbook was turning his life around.

Alisson's story is just one of many that prove how powerful a well-balanced diet can be in managing Parkinson's Disease. This cookbook had given him a renewed sense of hope, and he cherished every moment of his newfound vitality.

CHAPTER ONE

UNDERSTANDING PARKINSON'S DISEASE

What is Parkinson's Disease?

Parkinson's disease is a neurodegenerative condition largely affecting the central nervous system. It is typified by the progressive death of particular brain cells, which results in a lack of dopamine, a neurotransmitter essential for controlling movement and muscular function.

While there is no cure for Parkinson's Disease, various treatments, including medications, physical therapy, and deep brain stimulation, can help manage the symptoms.

Moreover, a well-balanced diet, as highlighted in the "Parkinson's Diet Cookbook for Seniors," can complement treatment strategies by providing essential nutrients to support brain health and overall well-being. By understanding the disease and adopting a suitable regimen, individuals with Parkinson's can lead fuller and more functional lives.

Common Symptoms Of Parkinson's in Seniors

Common symptoms of Parkinson's disease in seniors include a range of motor and non-motor issues. The hallmark motor symptoms encompass:

Tremors: Involuntary shaking, often beginning in the hands and fingers, which can affect daily tasks like writing or eating.

Bradykinesia: Slowness in initiating and completing movements, leading to a reduction in spontaneous physical activities.

Muscle Rigidity: Stiffness in the arms, legs, or neck, resulting in limited range of motion and discomfort.

Postural Instability: Difficulty in maintaining balance and an increased risk of falls, as seniors may experience unsteadiness.

Non-motor symptoms involve:

Depression: A sense of hopelessness and persistent sadness, which can affect the overall quality of life.

Sleep Disturbances: Issues like insomnia, restless leg syndrome, or vivid dreams can contribute to fatigue and decreased sleep quality.

Cognitive Impairment: Problems with memory, attention, and other cognitive functions are often part of the disease's progression.

These symptoms can vary in severity and progression from person to person. Understanding these common signs of Parkinson's in seniors is crucial for early diagnosis and appropriate management, as well as for the utilization of tools like dietary choices outlined in the "Parkinson's Diet Cookbook for Seniors" to help alleviate the disease's impact.

Treatment Approaches and Medications

Treatment approaches for Parkinson's disease in seniors aim to manage symptoms and improve overall quality of life. While there's no cure, various medications and therapies can help. Some common approaches include:

Medications: Levodopa is a primary medication, which the body converts into dopamine, a neurotransmitter lacking in Parkinson's patients. Dopamine agonists, MAO-B inhibitors, and anticholinergics are examples of other drugs.

Physical Therapy: Physical therapists can assist seniors with exercises to improve mobility, balance, and posture. This helps manage motor symptoms.

Occupational Therapy: Occupational therapists help seniors adapt their daily routines and environments to minimize difficulties caused by motor and non-motor symptoms.

Speech Therapy: Speech therapists work with patients to address speech and swallowing issues, common in advanced stages of the disease.

Deep Brain Stimulation (DBS): Surgical procedures like DBS may be considered in advanced cases to regulate abnormal brain activity.

Dietary and Nutritional Approaches: Dietary choices play a vital role in managing Parkinson's symptoms. Certain foods and nutrients can help alleviate motor and non-motor symptoms.

Importance of Nutrition in Managing Symptoms

Proper nutrition plays a pivotal role in managing the symptoms of Parkinson's disease in seniors. The importance of nutrition lies in its ability to address both motor and non-motor symptoms and improve overall quality of life. Here's why nutrition is vital:

Supports Medication Effectiveness: Certain foods can enhance the absorption and effectiveness of medications used to manage Parkinson's symptoms. For example, taking levodopa with a low-protein meal helps increase its absorption, reducing motor symptoms.

Balances Dopamine Levels: Nutrition can impact dopamine production in the brain.

Consuming foods rich in amino acids like tyrosine, a precursor to dopamine, can help maintain balanced dopamine levels.

Alleviates Non-Motor Symptoms: Constipation, mood disturbances, and cognitive issues are common non-motor symptoms in Parkinson's. A well-rounded diet with fiber, antioxidants, and omega-3 fatty acids can help address these problems.

Energy and Weight Management: Proper nutrition provides the energy needed to combat fatigue and maintain a healthy weight, preventing frailty and muscle loss.

Antioxidants and Anti-Inflammatory Properties: Nutrient-rich foods high in antioxidants and anti-inflammatory compounds can help reduce oxidative stress and inflammation, common in Parkinson's.

Foods to Eat and Avoid in Your Diet

When it comes to Parkinson's disease, diet plays a crucial role in managing symptoms and improving overall well-being for seniors. Here's a breakdown of foods to eat and avoid in your diet:

Foods to Eat:

Fruits and Vegetables: Rich in antioxidants, vitamins, and fiber, fruits and vegetables can help combat oxidative stress and inflammation. Leafy greens, berries, and vibrant fruit are very healthy.

Lean Proteins: Include protein sources that are low in fat, such as fish, chicken, legumes, and tofu. While protein is necessary, use low-fat options to reduce potential interactions with levodopa therapy.

Whole Grains: Whole grains, such as oats, brown rice, and whole wheat, offer a steady source of fiber and energy. They may also support the upkeep of a healthy digestive system.

Healthy Fats: Consume foods high in unsaturated fats, such as nuts, avocados, and olive oil. These fats support brain health and can help with cognitive function.

Probiotics: Fermented foods like yogurt, kefir, and sauerkraut can help maintain gut health, which is increasingly recognized as a factor in Parkinson's disease management.

Foods to Avoid:

Excessive Protein: While protein is important, excessive consumption can interfere with levodopa absorption. Be mindful of the timing of high-protein meals.

Saturated and Trans Fats: Limit saturated and trans fats found in fried foods, processed snacks, and certain animal products as they can contribute to inflammation.

Sugary and Processed Foods: High sugar intake and processed foods can worsen inflammation, impair energy levels, and contribute to weight issues.

Excess Salt: Sodium can affect blood pressure and lead to dehydration. High blood pressure can be detrimental for those with Parkinson's disease.

Caffeine: Caffeine can interfere with sleep patterns, leading to increased fatigue. Reduce your caffeine intake, particularly at night.

Seniors with Parkinson's disease can benefit significantly from a well-balanced diet that emphasizes whole, nutrient-dense foods while minimizing processed, high-fat, and high-sugar options.

Tips for Safe and Enjoyable Cooking

Cooking can be a therapeutic and enjoyable part of daily life, even for seniors with Parkinson's disease. To make the experience safe and delightful, here are some essential tips:

Adaptive Tools: Invest in adaptive kitchen tools and utensils, such as weighted or easy-grip utensils, to enhance dexterity and reduce the risk of spills.

Anti-Fatigue Mat: Use an anti-fatigue mat in the kitchen to minimize the impact on joints and provide added comfort while standing.

Simple Recipes: Opt for simple, Parkinson 's-friendly recipes from the cookbook, focusing on easy-to-follow steps and limited preparation time.

Pre-Chopped Ingredients: Buy pre-chopped or pre-washed ingredients to save time and effort in food preparation.

Steady Work Surface: Ensure a stable, non-slip work surface for chopping, cutting, and meal assembly.

Timer Reminders: Set timers to help manage cooking times, reducing the risk of burnt or overcooked dishes.

Be Mindful of Heat: Use induction stoves or appliances with safety features like automatic shut-off, preventing accidental burns.

Assistance: Don't hesitate to ask for assistance or cook with a friend or family member when needed.

These tips will empower seniors with Parkinson's to continue cooking and enjoying delicious, nutritious meals while minimizing the challenges posed by the disease. The "Parkinson's Disease Diet Cookbook for Seniors" offers valuable insights and recipes tailored to their unique needs.

CHAPTER TWO

BREAKFAST RECIPES

Spinach and Feta Breakfast Quesadilla

Serving: 1

Cooking Time: 15 minutes

Ingredients:

•1 whole-wheat tortilla

•1/4 cup baby spinach

•2 tbsp crumbled feta cheese

•2 large eggs

•Salt and pepper to taste

Preparation:

1. Place the whole-wheat tortilla on a clean, flat surface.

2. In a bowl, whisk the eggs and season with salt and pepper.

3. Heat a non-stick skillet over medium heat, then pour the whisked eggs into the pan.

4. As the eggs begin to set, add the baby spinach and feta cheese.

5. Once the eggs are fully cooked, place the egg, spinach, and feta mixture on half of the tortilla.

6. Fold the other half of the tortilla over to create a quesadilla.

7. Carefully transfer it back to the skillet and cook for an additional 2 minutes until it's golden brown and crispy on both sides.

8. Slice into wedges and serve.

Nutritional Value:

Calories: 325

Protein: 20g

Carbs: 22g

Fat: 17g

Banana Walnut Pancakes

Serving: 1

Cooking Time: 20 minutes

Ingredients:

•1 ripe banana, mashed

•1/4 cup chopped walnuts

•1/4 cup old-fashioned oats

•2 large eggs

•1/2 tsp cinnamon

•1/2 tsp vanilla extract

•Cooking spray

Preparation:

1. In a bowl, combine the mashed banana, chopped walnuts, old-fashioned oats, eggs, cinnamon, and vanilla extract. Mix until well combined.

2. Heat a non-stick skillet over medium heat and lightly grease with cooking spray.

3. Pour a portion of the pancake batter onto the skillet to form a pancake.

4. Cook for 2-3 minutes on each side until the pancake is golden brown and cooked through.

5. Repeat with the remaining batter to make additional pancakes and Serve.

Nutritional Value:

Calories: 455

Protein: 16g

Carbs: 37g

Fat: 28g

Blueberry Almond Oatmeal

Serving: 1

Cooking Time: 10 minutes

Ingredients:

- 1/2 cup rolled oats
- 1 cup unsweetened almond milk
- 1/2 cup blueberries (fresh or frozen)
- 1 tbsp almond butter
- 1 tsp honey
- Sliced almonds for garnish

Preparation:

1. In a saucepan, combine the rolled oats and almond milk.

2. Heat over medium heat and stir occasionally until the mixture thickens (about 5-7 minutes).

3. Once the oats are cooked, stir in the blueberries.

4. Transfer to a serving bowl, then drizzle with almond butter, honey, and garnish with sliced almonds.

Nutritional Value:
Calories: 370
Protein: 10g
Carbs: 51g
Fat: 14g

Mushroom and Spinach Omelet

Serving: 1
Cooking Time: 15 minutes

Ingredients:

•2 large eggs

•1/4 cup sliced mushrooms

•1/2 cup fresh spinach leaves

•2 tbsp grated Parmesan cheese

•Salt and pepper to taste

•Cooking spray

Preparation:

1. In a bowl, whisk the eggs and add a pinch of salt and pepper.

2. Heat a non-stick skillet over medium heat and lightly grease with cooking spray.

3. Pour the whisked eggs into the skillet.

4. Add the sliced mushrooms and fresh spinach on one side of the omelet.

5. Once the omelet is nearly set, sprinkle with Parmesan cheese and fold it in half.

6. Cook for another minute or until the cheese is melted and the omelet is cooked through.

Nutritional Value:

Calories: 286

Protein: 23g

Carbs: 5g

Fat: 19g

Protein-Packed Greek Yogurt Bowl

Serving: 1

Cooking Time: 5 minutes

Ingredients:

•1 cup Greek yogurt

•1/2 cup mixed berries (e.g., strawberries, raspberries, blueberries)

•2 tbsp honey

•1/4 cup granola

Preparation:

1. In a serving bowl, add Greek yogurt as the base. Top with mixed berries.

2. Drizzle honey over the berries.

3. Sprinkle granola for added crunch.

Nutritional Value:
Calories: 360
Protein: 22g
Carbs: 46g
Fat: 11g

Buckwheat Pancakes with Berries

Serving: 1

Cooking Time: 20 minutes

Ingredients:

- 1/2 cup buckwheat flour
- 1/2 cup almond milk
- 1 large egg
- 1/2 tsp baking powder
- 1/2 tsp vanilla extract
- 1/2 cup mixed berries
- 1 tbsp maple syrup

Preparation:

1. In a mixing bowl, combine the buckwheat flour, almond milk, egg, baking powder, and vanilla extract. Mix until well combined.

2. Heat a non-stick skillet over medium heat and lightly grease with cooking spray.

3. Pour the pancake batter onto the skillet to form pancakes.

4. Cook until bubbles appear on top, then turn and continue cooking until the other side becomes golden brown. Serve and Enjoy!

Nutritional Value:
Calories: 430
Protein: 13g
Carbs: 77g
Fat: 7g

Sweet Potato Hash

Serving: 1
Cooking Time: 25 minutes

Ingredients:
•1 medium sweet potato, peeled and diced

•1/2 small onion, chopped

•1/2 red bell pepper, diced

•1/2 tsp paprika

•Salt and pepper to taste

•1 tbsp olive oil

Preparation:

1. Heat olive oil in a skillet over medium heat.

2. Add chopped onion and red bell pepper and sauté until softened.

3. Add diced sweet potato and season with paprika, salt, and pepper.

4. Cook while stirring frequently until the sweet potatoes are tender and slightly crispy. Serve!

Nutritional Value:

Calories: 380

Protein: 4g

Carbs: 62g

Fat: 15g

CHAPTER THREE

SNACK RECIPES

Homemade Veggie Chips

Serving: 1

Preparation Time: 10 minutes

Ingredients:

•1 medium sweet potato

•1 small beetroot

•1 zucchini

•1 tbsp olive oil

•Salt and pepper to taste

Preparation:

1. Preheat the oven to 375°F (190°C).

2. Wash and peel the sweet potato, beetroot, and zucchini.

3. Use a mandoline slicer or a knife to slice the vegetables thinly.

4. Place the sliced veggies in a mixing bowl, drizzle with olive oil, and season with salt and pepper. Toss to coat.

5. Arrange the veggie slices on a baking sheet in a single layer.

6. Bake the chips for 15-20 minutes, or until they become crisp. Keep a watchful eye on them to avoid scorching.

7. Allow the chips to cool before enjoying.

Nutritional Value:

Calories: 180

Protein: 2g

Carbs: 22g

Fat: 10g

Almond Butter and Banana Rice Cakes

Serving: 1
Preparation Time: 5 minutes

Ingredients:

•2 rice cakes

•2 tbsp almond butter

•1 small banana, sliced

•Honey (optional)

Preparation:

1. Spread almond butter evenly on each rice cake.

2. Top with banana slices.

3. Drizzle with honey if desired. Enjoy!

Nutritional Value:

Calories: 280

Protein: 5g

Carbs: 34g

Fat: 14g

Cranberry and Walnut Trail Mix

Serving: 1

Preparation Time: 5 minutes

Ingredients:

1/4 cup dried cranberries

1/4 cup walnuts

1/4 cup almonds

1/4 cup sunflower seeds

Preparation:

1. Combine all the ingredients in a small bowl.

2. Toss to mix. Your trail mix is ready to enjoy.

Nutritional Value:

Calories: 350

Protein: 8g

Carbs: 20g

Fat: 28g

Quinoa and Veggie Muffins

Serving: 1

Preparation Time: 30 minutes

Ingredients:
•1/2 cup cooked quinoa
•1/4 cup grated zucchini
•1/4 cup grated carrot
•2 eggs
•1/4 cup grated cheese (optional)
•Salt and pepper to taste

Preparation:

1. Preheat the oven to 350°F (175°C).

2. In a mixing bowl, combine quinoa, grated zucchini, grated carrot, eggs, and grated cheese if desired.

3. Season with salt and pepper.

4. Grease a muffin tin or use silicone muffin cups.

5. Divide the mixture into the muffin cups.

6. Bake for 20-25 minutes or until the muffins are set.

7. Allow to cool before serving.

Nutritional Value:

Calories: 250

Protein: 14g

Carbs: 16g

Fat: 15g

Cottage Cheese and Sliced Peaches

Serving: 1

Preparation Time: 5 minutes

Ingredients:

•1/2 cup low-fat cottage cheese

•1 ripe peach, sliced

•Honey (optional)

Preparation:

1. Spoon cottage cheese into a bowl.

2. Top with sliced peaches.

3. Drizzle with honey if desired.

Nutritional Value:

Calories: 190

Protein: 15g

Carbs: 30g

Fat: 2g

Cucumber Dill Bites

Serving: 1

Preparation Time: 10 minutes

Ingredients:

•1 cucumber, sliced

•1/2 cup low-fat Greek yogurt

•1 tsp fresh dill, chopped

•Salt and pepper to taste

Preparation:

1. In a bowl, mix Greek yogurt with fresh dill, salt, and pepper.

2. Spread a small amount of the yogurt mixture on each cucumber slice. Serve!

Nutritional Value:

Calories: 90

Protein: 8g

Carbs: 12g

Fat: 1g

Mini Salmon Cakes with Lemon Aioli

Serving: 1

Preparation Time: 25 minutes

Ingredients for Salmon Cakes:

•4 oz canned salmon, drained and flaked

•1/4 cup whole-grain breadcrumbs

•1/4 cup diced red bell pepper

•1/4 cup diced green onions

•1 egg

•1 tsp lemon juice

•Salt and pepper to taste

•Olive oil for cooking

Ingredients for Lemon Aioli:

•2 tbsp Greek yogurt

•1/2 tsp lemon juice

•1/4 tsp garlic powder

•Salt and pepper to taste

Preparation:

1. In a mixing bowl, combine salmon, breadcrumbs, red bell pepper, green onions, egg, lemon juice, salt, and pepper.

2. Form the mixture into small patties.

3. Heat olive oil in a skillet and cook the salmon cakes for about 4 minutes on each side or until golden brown.

4. In a separate bowl, mix Greek yogurt, lemon juice, garlic powder, salt, and pepper to prepare the aioli. Serve!

Nutritional Value:

Calories: 360

Protein: 26g

Carbs: 26g

Fat: 16g

CHAPTER FOUR

LUNCH RECIPES

Turkey and Cranberry Spinach Salad

Serving: 1
Preparation Time: 15 minutes

Ingredients:

- 2 cups fresh spinach
- 3 oz cooked turkey breast, sliced
- 1/4 cup dried cranberries
- 2 tbsp chopped pecans
- 1 tbsp balsamic vinaigrette

Preparation:

1. Place fresh spinach in a bowl.

2. Top with sliced turkey, dried cranberries, and chopped pecans.

3. Drizzle with balsamic vinaigrette.

4. Toss and enjoy this delightful salad.

Nutritional Value:

Calories: 380

Protein: 20g

Carbs: 40g

Fat: 16g

Vegetable and Lentil Soup

Serving: 1

Preparation Time: 30 minutes

Ingredients:

•1/2 cup dried green lentils

•1 cup mixed vegetables (carrots, celery, onions)

•1 clove garlic, minced

•4 cups vegetable broth

•1 tsp olive oil

•Salt and pepper to taste

Preparation:

1. In a pot, heat olive oil, then add minced garlic and mixed vegetables. Sauté until slightly softened.

2. Rinse lentils and add them to the pot along with vegetable broth.

3. Bring to a boil, then reduce heat and let it simmer for about 25 minutes.

4. Season with salt and pepper to taste. Serve

Nutritional Value:

Calories: 350

Protein: 18g

Carbs: 60g

Fat: 3g

Quinoa-Stuffed Bell Peppers

Serving: 1

Preparation Time: 45 minutes

Ingredients:

•1 bell pepper

•1/2 cup cooked quinoa

•1/4 cup black beans

•1/4 cup diced tomatoes

•1/4 cup chopped spinach

•1/4 tsp chili powder

•1/4 tsp cumin

•Salt and pepper to taste

Preparation:

1. Preheat the oven to 375°F (190°C).

2. Cut the top off the bell pepper and remove the seeds.

3. In a bowl, combine cooked quinoa, black beans, diced tomatoes, chopped spinach, chili powder, cumin, salt, and pepper.

4. Stuff the mixture into the bell pepper.

5. Place the stuffed pepper in a baking dish and cover with aluminum foil.

6. Bake for about 30 minutes or until the pepper is tender. Enjoy!

Nutritional Value:
Calories: 350
Protein: 12g
Carbs: 68g
Fat: 5g

Creamy Avocado Tuna Salad

Serving: 1

Preparation Time: 10 minutes

Ingredients:

•1/2 ripe avocado, mashed

•3 oz canned tuna in water, drained

•1/4 cup diced cucumber

•1/4 cup diced red bell pepper

•1 tbsp Greek yogurt

•1 tsp lemon juice

•Salt and pepper to taste

Preparation:

1. In a bowl, mix mashed avocado, drained tuna, diced cucumber, and diced red bell pepper.

2. Add Greek yogurt, lemon juice, salt, and pepper, and mix well. Enjoy!

Nutritional Value:

Calories: 320

Protein: 25g

Carbs: 15g

Fat: 18g

Sweet Potato and Chickpea Curry

Serving: 1

Preparation Time: 30 minutes

Ingredients:

•1 small sweet potato, peeled and cubed

•1/2 cup canned chickpeas, drained

•1/4 cup diced onion

•1/4 cup diced tomatoes

•1/4 cup canned coconut milk

•1 tsp olive oil

•1/2 tsp curry powder

•Salt and pepper to taste

Preparation:

1. In a pan, heat olive oil, then add diced onion and sauté until translucent.

2. Add sweet potato cubes, diced tomatoes, chickpeas, coconut milk, curry powder, salt, and pepper.

3. Let it simmer until the sweet potatoes are tender and the curry thickens. Serve and Enjoy!

Nutritional Value:
Calories: 400
Protein: 10g
Carbs: 60g
Fat: 14g

Spinach and Mushroom Quiche

Serving: 1

Preparation Time: 40 minutes

Ingredients:

- 1/2 cup fresh spinach, chopped
- 1/4 cup sliced mushrooms
- 2 large eggs
- 1/4 cup milk
- 1/4 cup shredded cheddar cheese
- Salt and pepper to taste

Preparation:

1. Preheat the oven to 350°F (180°C).

2. In a bowl, beat eggs, then add milk, spinach, sliced mushrooms, shredded cheddar cheese, salt, and pepper.

3. Transfer the blend onto a pie dish that has been lightly coated with grease.

4. Bake for about 30 minutes or until set. Enjoy!

Nutritional Value:
Calories: 350
Protein: 18g
Carbs: 10g
Fat: 25g

Greek-Style Zucchini Noodles

Serving: 1
Preparation Time: 20 minutes

Ingredients:
•1 medium zucchini, spiralized
•1/4 cup diced cucumber
•1/4 cup diced tomatoes
•1/4 cup crumbled feta cheese

•1 tbsp olive oil

•1 tsp lemon juice

•Fresh dill and black olives for garnish

Preparation:

1. In a bowl, toss zucchini noodles, diced cucumber, and diced tomatoes.

2. Spoon on a bit of lemon juice and olive oil.

3. Top with crumbled feta cheese, fresh dill, and black olives. Enjoy!

Nutritional Value:

Calories: 300

Protein: 8g

Carbs: 15g

Fat: 22g

CHAPTER FIVE

DINNER RECIPES

Lemon and Herb Roasted Chicken

Serving: 1

Cooking Time: 40 minutes

Ingredients:

•1 boneless, skinless chicken breast

•1/2 lemon, juiced

•1 tsp olive oil

•1/2 tsp dried herbs (thyme, rosemary, oregano)

•Salt and pepper to taste

Preparation:

1. Preheat the oven to 375°F (190°C).

2. In a bowl, mix lemon juice, olive oil, dried herbs, salt, and pepper.

3. Apply the mixture to the chicken breast.

4. Bake for about 30-35 minutes until the chicken is cooked through. Enjoy!

Nutritional Value:
Calories: 350
Protein: 40g
Carbs: 2g
Fat: 20g

Vegetable Stir-Fry with Tofu

Serving: 1
Cooking Time: 20 minutes

Ingredients:
•1/2 cup tofu, cubed

•1 cup mixed stir-fry vegetables (broccoli, bell peppers, carrots)
•1 tbsp low-sodium soy sauce
•1/2 tsp ginger, minced
•1/2 tsp garlic, minced
•1 tsp sesame oil

Preparation:

1. In a pan, stir-fry tofu until golden brown.

2. Add mixed vegetables, soy sauce, minced ginger, and minced garlic.

3. Stir-fry until vegetables are tender.

4. Drizzle with sesame oil and serve.

Nutritional Value:
Calories: 300
Protein: 15g
Carbs: 20g

Fat: 15g

Grilled Salmon with Dill Sauce

Serving: 1

Cooking Time: 15 minutes

Ingredients:

•1 salmon fillet

•1/4 cup Greek yogurt

•1/2 tsp fresh dill, chopped

•1/2 lemon, juiced

•Salt and pepper to taste

Preparation:

1. Preheat the grill.

2. Season the salmon fillet with salt and pepper.

3. Grill for about 10 minutes until the salmon is cooked.

4. In a small bowl, mix Greek yogurt, fresh dill, and lemon juice.

5. Drizzle dill sauce over the grilled salmon.

Nutritional Value:

Calories: 350

Protein: 35g

Carbs: 6g

Fat: 20g

Veggie and Bean Chili

Serving: 1

Cooking Time: 30 minutes

Ingredients:

•1/2 cup mixed beans (kidney, black, pinto)

•1/2 cup diced tomatoes

•1/4 cup diced bell peppers

•1/4 cup diced onion

•1 tsp chili powder

•Salt and pepper to taste

Preparation:

1. In a pot, combine mixed beans, diced tomatoes, diced bell peppers, diced onion, and chili powder.

2. Season with salt and pepper.

3. Simmer for about 20 minutes until the chili thickens. Serve and Enjoy!

Nutritional Value:

Calories: 300

Protein: 10g

Carbs: 50g

Fat: 5g

Turkey and Kale Sauté

Serving: 1

Cooking Time: 20 minutes

Ingredients:

- 1/2 cup ground turkey
- 1 cup kale leaves, chopped
- 1/4 cup diced onion
- 1/4 cup diced tomatoes
- 1/2 tsp garlic powder
- Salt and pepper to taste

Preparation:

1. In a skillet, cook ground turkey until browned.

2. Add diced onion, diced tomatoes, chopped kale, garlic powder, salt, and pepper.

3. Sauté until kale wilts. Enjoy!

Nutritional Value:

Calories: 320

Protein: 25g

Carbs: 10g

Fat: 15g

Baked Cod with Garlic and Herbs

Serving: 1

Cooking Time: 25 minutes

Ingredients:

•1 cod fillet

•1 tsp olive oil

•1/2 tsp minced garlic

•1/2 tsp dried herbs (parsley, thyme, rosemary)

•Salt and pepper to taste

Preparation:

1. Preheat the oven to 350°F (180°C).

2. Set aside a baking sheet for the cod fillet.

3. Drizzle with olive oil, minced garlic, dried herbs, salt, and pepper.

4. Bake for about 15-20 minutes until the cod flakes easily. Enjoy!

Nutritional Value:

Calorics: 280

Protein: 30g

Carbs: 2g

Fat: 10g

Cauliflower and Chickpea Stew

Serving: 1

Cooking Time: 30 minutes

Ingredients:
- 1 cup cauliflower florets
- 1/2 cup canned chickpeas, drained
- 1/4 cup diced tomatoes
- 1/4 cup diced onion
- 1/2 tsp curry powder
- Salt and pepper to taste

Preparation:

1. In a pot, combine cauliflower florets, canned chickpeas, diced tomatoes, diced onion, curry powder, salt, and pepper.

2. Simmer for about 20-25 minutes until cauliflower is tender. Serve!

CHAPTER SIX

SIDES

Cilantro Lime Quinoa

Serving: 1
Cooking Time: 15 minutes

Ingredients:

- 1/2 cup quinoa
- 1 cup water
- 1/4 cup fresh cilantro, chopped
- Juice of 1/2 lime
- Salt and pepper to taste

Preparation:

1. Rinse quinoa under cold water.

2. In a saucepan, combine quinoa and water. Bring to a boil.

3. Reduce heat, cover, and simmer for about 12 minutes.

4. Fluff-cooked quinoa with a fork.

5. Mix in chopped cilantro, lime juice, salt, and pepper. Enjoy this zesty quinoa.

Nutritional Value:
Calories: 220
Protein: 5g
Carbs: 40g
Fat: 3g

Steamed Broccoli with Garlic

Serving: 1

Cooking Time: 10 minutes

Ingredients:

- 1 cup broccoli florets
- 1 clove garlic, minced
- 1/2 tsp olive oil
- Salt and pepper to taste

Preparation:

1. Steam broccoli florets until tender, about 5-7 minutes.

2. In a skillet, heat olive oil and sauté minced garlic until fragrant.

3. Toss steamed broccoli with garlic, salt, and pepper. Enjoy!

Nutritional Value:

Calories: 70

Protein: 3g

Carbs: 10g

Fat: 2g

Butternut Squash and Apple Bake

Serving: 1
Cooking Time: 30 minutes

Ingredients:

•1 cup butternut squash, cubed

•1 apple, sliced

•1/2 tsp cinnamon

•1 tsp honey

Preparation:

1. Preheat the oven to 375°F (190°C).

2. Toss butternut squash and apple with cinnamon and honey.

3. Bake for about 25-30 minutes until tender and golden. Enjoy this sweet and savory bake.

Nutritional Value:
Calories: 250
Protein: 2g
Carbs: 60g
Fat: 1g

Lemon Garlic Asparagus

Serving: 1
Cooking Time: 15 minutes

Ingredients:
•1 cup asparagus spears
•1/2 lemon, juiced
•1 clove garlic, minced

•1/2 tsp olive oil

•Salt and pepper to taste

Preparation:

1. Steam asparagus spears until tender, about 5-7 minutes.

2. In a skillet, heat olive oil and sauté minced garlic until fragrant.

3. Toss steamed asparagus with lemon juice, garlic, salt, and pepper. Enjoy!

Nutritional Value:

Calories: 80

Protein: 3g

Carbs: 15g

Fat: 2g

Mashed Sweet Potatoes with Cinnamon

Serving: 1

Cooking Time: 20 minutes

Ingredients:

•1 sweet potato, peeled and cubed

•1/2 tsp cinnamon

•1/2 tsp honey

•Salt to taste

Preparation:

1. Boil sweet potato cubes until tender, about 10-12 minutes.

2. Drain and mash sweet potatoes.

3. Mix in cinnamon, honey, and a pinch of salt.

Nutritional Value:

Calories: 180

Protein: 2g

Carbs: 45g

Fat: 0.5g

Tomato and Cucumber Salad

Serving: 1

Cooking Time: 10 minutes

Ingredients:

•1 tomato, diced

•1/2 cucumber, sliced

•1/4 cup red onion, thinly sliced

•1 tbsp balsamic vinegar

•Salt and pepper to taste

Preparation:

1. In a bowl, combine diced tomato, sliced cucumber, and thinly sliced red onion.

2. Drizzle with balsamic vinegar and season with salt and pepper.

3. Toss to mix and serve this fresh salad.

Nutritional Value:
Calories: 70
Protein: 2g
Carbs: 15g
Fat: 0.5g

Baked Brown Rice

Serving: 1
Cooking Time: 45 minutes

Ingredients:
•1/2 cup brown rice
•1 cup water
•1/2 tsp olive oil

Preparation:

1. Preheat the oven to 375°F (190°C).

2. In a baking dish, combine brown rice and water.

3. Drizzle with olive oil and cover tightly with foil.

4. Bake for about 45-50 minutes until rice is tender and water is absorbed.

5. Fluff the baked brown rice with a fork.

Nutritional Value:

Calories: 220

Protein: 5g

Carbs: 45g

Fat: 2g

CHAPTER SEVEN

SOUPS & STEWS

Creamy Butternut Squash Soup

Serving: 1

Cooking Time: 40 minutes

Ingredients:

- 1 cup butternut squash, peeled and cubed
- 1/2 cup vegetable broth
- 1/4 cup coconut milk
- 1/2 tsp nutmeg
- Salt and pepper to taste

Preparation:

1. In a pot, combine butternut squash, vegetable broth, coconut milk, and nutmeg.

2. Simmer until squash is tender.

3. Blend until creamy. Season with salt and pepper. Enjoy!

Nutritional Value:
Calories: 180
Protein: 3g
Carbs: 25g
Fat: 8g

Classic Chicken Noodle Soup

Serving: 1
Cooking Time: 30 minutes

Ingredients:
- 1/2 cup cooked chicken, shredded
- 1/2 cup cooked noodles
- 2 cups chicken broth
- 1/2 cup mixed vegetables
- Salt and pepper to taste

Preparation:

1. In a pot, combine chicken, cooked noodles, chicken broth, and mixed vegetables.

2. Simmer until vegetables are tender.

3. Season with salt and pepper. Enjoy!

Nutritional Value:

Calories: 280

Protein: 15g

Carbs: 25g

Fat: 12g

Hearty Vegetable and Barley Stew

Serving: 1

Cooking Time: 45 minutes

Ingredients:

•1/4 cup pearl barley

•1 cup vegetable broth

•1/2 cup mixed vegetables

•1/2 cup cooked beans

•1/2 tsp thyme

Preparation:

1. In a pot, combine pearl barley, vegetable broth, mixed vegetables, cooked beans, and thyme.

2. Simmer until barley is tender. Enjoy!

Nutritional Value:

Calories: 260

Protein: 7g

Carbs: 54g

Fat: 1g

Tomato Basil Bisque

Serving: 1

Cooking Time: 25 minutes

Ingredients:

•1 cup tomato soup

•1/4 cup fresh basil leaves

•1/4 cup Greek yogurt

•A sprinkle of black pepper

Preparation:

1. Heat tomato soup.

2. In a blender, combine tomato soup, fresh basil leaves, Greek yogurt, and black pepper.

3. Blend until smooth.

Nutritional Value:

Calories: 160

Protein: 7g

Carbs: 20g

Fat: 6g

Mediterranean Lentil Soup

Serving: 1
Cooking Time: 40 minutes

Ingredients:

•1/4 cup lentils

•1 cup vegetable broth

•1/4 cup diced tomatoes

•1/4 cup chopped spinach

•1/2 tsp cumin

Preparation:

1. In a pot, combine lentils, vegetable broth, diced tomatoes, chopped spinach, and cumin.

2. Simmer until lentils are cooked. Enjoy!

Nutritional Value:

Calories: 240

Protein: 15g

Carbs: 40g

Fat: 1.5g

Spinach and White Bean Minestrone

Serving: 1

Cooking Time: 35 minutes

Ingredients:

- 1/4 cup cooked white beans
- 1/4 cup chopped spinach
- 1/4 cup diced tomatoes
- 1/4 cup vegetable broth

•1/2 tsp Italian seasoning

Preparation:

1. In a pot, combine white beans, chopped spinach, diced tomatoes, vegetable broth, and Italian seasoning.

2. Simmer until heated through. Enjoy!

Nutritional Value:
Calories: 220
Protein: 8g
Carbs: 38g
Fat: 1g

Creamy Mushroom Bisque

Serving: 1
Cooking Time: 30 minutes

Ingredients:

•1 cup mushroom soup

•1/4 cup chopped mushrooms

•1/4 cup coconut milk

•Salt and pepper to taste

Preparation:

1. Heat mushroom soup.

2. In a pan, sauté chopped mushrooms until tender.

3. Add sautéed mushrooms and coconut milk to the soup. Season with salt and pepper. Enjoy!

Nutritional Value:

Calories: 190

Protein: 5g

Carbs: 16g

Fat: 12g

CHAPTER EIGHT

DESSERT RECIPES

Berry Parfait with Greek Yogurt

Serving: 1
Cooking Time: 10 minutes

Ingredients:
- 1/2 cup Greek yogurt
- 1/4 cup mixed berries
- 1 tbsp honey
- A sprinkle of granola

Preparation:

1. In a glass, layer Greek yogurt, mixed berries, and honey.

2. Top with a sprinkle of granola. Enjoy!

Nutritional Value:

Calories: 200

Protein: 10g

Carbs: 30g

Fat: 5g

Baked Apples with Walnuts and Cinnamon

Serving: 1

Cooking Time: 30 minutes

Ingredients:

•1 apple, cored and sliced

•1 tbsp crushed walnuts

•1/2 tsp cinnamon

•1/2 tsp honey

Preparation:

1. Preheat the oven to 375°F (190°C).

2. In an oven-safe dish, place apple slices.

3.   Sprinkle   it   with   crushed   walnuts, cinnamon, and drizzle honey.

4. Bake for about 20-25 minutes until apples are tender.

Nutritional Value:

Calories: 180

Protein: 2g

Carbs: 40g

Fat: 4g

Chocolate-Dipped Strawberries

Serving: 1

Cooking Time: 15 minutes

Ingredients:

•5 strawberries

•1 oz dark chocolate, melted

Preparation:

1. Dip strawberries into melted dark chocolate.

2. Place them on parchment paper to cool and harden. Enjoy!

Nutritional Value:

Calories: 150

Protein: 1g

Carbs: 15g

Fat: 9g

Mango and Pineapple Sorbet

Serving: 1

Preparation Time: 5 minutes

Ingredients:

•1 cup frozen mango chunks

•1/2 cup frozen pineapple chunks

•2 tbsp water

Preparation:

1. Blend frozen mango and pineapple with water until smooth.

2. Scoop and serve as a refreshing sorbet. Enjoy!

Nutritional Value:

Calories: 130

Protein: 1g

Carbs: 34g

Fat: 0.5g

Banana Nut Chia Pudding

Serving: 1

Preparation Time: 5 minutes

Ingredients:

- 1 ripe banana, mashed
- 2 tbsp chia seeds
- 1/2 cup almond milk

•1 tbsp chopped nuts (e.g., walnuts or almonds)

Preparation:

1. Mix mashed banana, chia seeds, and almond milk in a jar.

2. Refrigerate overnight.

3. Top with chopped nuts before serving. Enjoy!

Nutritional Value:
Calories: 250
Protein: 6g
Carbs: 34g
Fat: 11g

Fresh Berries with Whipped Cream

Serving: 1
Preparation Time: 5 minutes

Ingredients:
•1/2 cup mixed berries (e.g., strawberries, blueberries, raspberries)
•2 tbsp whipped cream
•1/2 tsp honey

Preparation:
1. Arrange mixed berries in a bowl.

2. Top with whipped cream and drizzle with honey. Enjoy!

Nutritional Value:
Calories: 120
Protein: 2g
Carbs: 20g

Fat: 4g

Creamy Avocado Chocolate Mousse

Serving: 1
Preparation Time: 10 minutes

Ingredients:

•1 ripe avocado

•2 tbsp cocoa powder

•1/2 tsp honey

•A pinch of salt

Preparation:

1. Blend ripe avocado, cocoa powder, honey, and a pinch of salt until smooth.

2. Serve as a luscious chocolate mousse. Enjoy!

Nutritional Value:

Calories: 220

Protein: 4g

Carbs: 18g.   Fats: 15g

7-DAY MEAL PLAN

Day 1

Breakfast: Banana Walnut Pancakes

Snack: Almond Butter and Banana Rice Cakes

Lunch: Vegetable and Lentil Soup

Snack: Cranberry and Walnut Trail Mix

Dinner: Grilled Salmon with Dill Sauce

Dessert: Chocolate-Dipped Strawberries

Day 2

Breakfast: Blueberry Almond Oatmeal

Snack: Homemade Veggie Chips

Lunch: Creamy Avocado Tuna Salad

Snack: Cottage Cheese and Sliced Peaches

Dinner: Vegetable Stir-Fry with Tofu

Dessert: Creamy Avocado Chocolate Mousse

Day 3

Breakfast: Mushroom and Spinach Omelette

Snack: Cucumber Dill Bites

Lunch: Sweet Potato and Chickpea Curry

Snack: Almond Butter and Banana Rice Cakes

Dinner: Baked Cod with Garlic and Herbs

Dessert: Fresh Berries with Whipped Cream

Day 4

Breakfast: Protein-Packed Greek Yogurt Bowl

Snack: Quinoa and Veggie Muffins

Lunch: Greek-style zucchini Noodles

Snack: Cranberry and Walnut Trail Mix

Dinner: Turkey and Cranberry Spinach Salad

Dessert: Banana Nut Chia Pudding

Day 5

Breakfast: Buckwheat Pancakes with Berries

Snack: Almond Butter and Banana Rice Cakes

Lunch: Spinach and Mushroom Quiche

Snack: Homemade Veggie Chips

Dinner: Veggie and Bean Chili

Dessert: Berry Parfait with Greek Yogurt

Day 6

Breakfast: Sweet Potato Hash

Snack: Cottage Cheese and Sliced Peaches

Lunch: Quinoa-stuffed bell Peppers

Snack: Cucumber Dill Bites

Dinner: Lemon and Herb Roasted Chicken

Dessert: Mango and Pineapple Sorbet

Day 7

Breakfast: Cilantro Lime Quinoa

Snack: Almond Butter and Banana Rice Cakes

Lunch: Classic Chicken Noodle Soup

Snack: Cranberry and Walnut Trail Mix

Dinner: Cauliflower and Chickpea Stew

Dessert: Fresh Berries with Whipped Cream

This meal plan offers a variety of delicious and nutritious meals that are tailored for seniors with Parkinson's disease. It ensures a balanced intake of essential nutrients while considering their dietary needs. Enjoy your meals while promoting overall well-being!

CONCLUSION

In conclusion, the "Parkinson's Disease Diet Cookbook for Seniors" is not just a collection of recipes; it's a lifeline to a healthier and more fulfilling life for those living with Parkinson's disease. We've taken into account the unique challenges and dietary requirements that seniors face, especially when dealing with this condition. Each recipe has been carefully crafted to provide essential nutrients, manage symptoms, and, most importantly, bring joy back to the dining table. Your journey to better health starts here. By embracing the recipes in this cookbook, you're not only nourishing your body but also nurturing your spirit. We understand the frustration and discomfort that Parkinson's disease can bring, and we want to be a part of your success story.

Remember, every meal you prepare from these pages is a powerful step toward managing your symptoms, improving your quality of life, and enhancing your overall well-being. As you embark on this culinary adventure, know that you're not alone. There's a community of individuals who have walked this path, found relief, and discovered renewed vitality through the foods you're about to savor.

So, to every reader, we leave you with this motivation: embrace this cookbook as more than a collection of recipes. Consider it your partner in the journey to a healthier, happier life. Don't just read these pages; let them inspire you to take action, adapt to this diet, and experience the transformative power of food in managing Parkinson's disease.
Your path to a more vibrant, fulfilling, and active life starts now.

The "Parkinson's Disease Diet Cookbook for Seniors" is your guide – your friend on this remarkable journey. Bon appétit!

www.ingramcontent.com/pod-product-compliance
Lightning Source LLC
Chambersburg PA
CBHW070832260726
48660CB00005B/2027